BLUEPRINT TO CASHING OUT CRYPTOCURRENCIES

Summary

1.   Cashing Out from Coinbase: A Step-by-Step Guide to Converting Your Crypto to Cash - This chapter provides a detailed guide on how to cash out from Coinbase, one of the most popular cryptocurrency exchanges. Readers will learn how to set up their account, complete identity verification, sell cryptocurrency, and withdraw funds to their bank account.
2.   How to Use LocalBitcoins to Find Buyers and Sell Your Crypto for Cash - This chapter explains how to use LocalBitcoins to find buyers and sell cryptocurrency for cash in a P2P manner. Readers will learn how to create an account, post a trade ad, and complete a trade safely.
3.   Cashing Out from Binance: Tips and Tricks for Withdrawing Your Profits - This chapter provides tips and tricks for withdrawing profits from Binance, one of the largest cryptocurrency exchanges. Readers will learn about the withdrawal process, fees, and limits, and how to maximize their profits.
4.   Converting Crypto to Cash with PayPal: A Safe and Secure Option for Small Transactions - This chapter discusses how to use PayPal to convert cryptocurrency to cash for small transactions. Readers will learn how to set up an account, link it to their cryptocurrency exchange, and complete a transaction.
5.   How to Sell Your Crypto for Cash on P2P Marketplaces like Paxful and Bisq - This chapter explains how to sell cryptocurrency for cash on P2P marketplaces like Paxful and Bisq. Readers will learn how to create an account, post a trade ad, and complete a trade safely.
6.   Cashing Out from Kraken: A Comprehensive Guide to Fiat Withdrawals - This chapter provides a comprehensive guide on how to withdraw fiat currency from Kraken, one of the oldest cryptocurrency exchanges. Readers will learn about the withdrawal process, fees, and limits, and how to maximize their profits.
7.   The Best Crypto Debit Cards for Instant Cash Withdrawals Anywhere in the World - This chapter discusses the best crypto debit cards for instant cash withdrawals anywhere in

the world. Readers will learn about the features, fees, and limits of different crypto debit cards and how to use them to withdraw cash.

8. Using Over-the-Counter (OTC) Trading Desks to Cash Out Large Amounts of Crypto - This chapter explains how to use over-the-counter (OTC) trading desks to cash out large amounts of cryptocurrency. Readers will learn about the benefits of using OTC trading desks, popular desks, and best practices for using them.

9. How to Avoid Common Scams and Frauds When Cashing Out Your Crypto - This chapter provides tips on how to avoid common scams and frauds when cashing out cryptocurrency. Readers will learn about common scams, how to spot them, and how to protect themselves from them.

10. Cashing Out Your Crypto for Cash at ATMs: A Beginner's Guide to Bitcoin ATMs and Their Limitations - This chapter provides a beginner's guide to Bitcoin ATMs and their limitations when cashing out cryptocurrency for cash. Readers will learn how to find and use Bitcoin ATMs, the fees and limits associated with their use, and their limitations.

11. The Pros and Cons of Cashing Out Crypto for Cash - This chapter discusses the pros and cons of cashing out cryptocurrency for cash. Readers will learn about the advantages and disadvantages of cashing out, how to choose the best method, and how to minimize the associated risks.

12. Tax Implications of Cashing Out Crypto for Cash - This chapter discusses the tax implications of cashing out cryptocurrency for cash. Readers will learn about the tax laws in different countries, how to calculate capital gains or losses, and how to minimize their tax liabilities.

Dedication

This book is dedicated to my mother Ms. N. Collins. Ty for encouraging me to never give up on my dreams. This book is also dedicated to my best friend N. A. Gibson who always encourages me to be great. Finally in dedication to all the Cryptologists who have questions about cashing out of cryptocurrencies and into cash. Thank you!

Introduction

Cryptocurrency has become a popular investment option, with the potential for high returns. However, cashing out cryptocurrency for cash can be a complex process. In this book, we provide a comprehensive guide to help you understand the process of cashing out cryptocurrency.

We cover various methods, including how to cash out from popular exchanges like Coinbase and Binance, and how to use P2P marketplaces like LocalBitcoins, Paxful, and Bisq. We also explore the benefits and drawbacks of cashing out to platforms like PayPal, crypto debit cards, and Bitcoin ATMs.

In addition, we discuss how to avoid common scams and frauds when cashing out and provide a comprehensive guide to tax implications of cashing out cryptocurrency for cash.

Whether you're new to the world of cryptocurrency or a seasoned investor, this book is a valuable resource for anyone looking to cash out their cryptocurrency for cash. By understanding the various methods and considerations involved, you can make informed decisions that help you achieve your financial goals in this dynamic and ever-evolving space.

CHAPTER 1

Cashing Out from Coinbase: A Step-by-Step Guide to Converting Your Crypto to Cash

Coinbase is one of the most popular cryptocurrency exchanges in the world, and it offers a user-friendly platform for buying, selling, and storing cryptocurrencies like Bitcoin, Ethereum, and Litecoin. If you're looking to cash out your cryptocurrency on Coinbase and convert it to cash, there are a few steps you need to follow.

STEP 1: SELL YOUR CRYPTOCURRENCY

The first step in cashing out your cryptocurrency on Coinbase is to sell your coins. To do this, you need to go to the "Sell" page on the Coinbase platform and select the cryptocurrency you want to sell. You can choose to sell all of your coins or just a portion of them.

STEP 2: CHOOSE YOUR PAYOUT METHOD

After you have sold your cryptocurrency, you will need to choose how you want to receive your payout. Coinbase offers several payout methods, including bank transfer, PayPal, and cryptocurrency. If you choose to receive your payout in cryptocurrency, you can transfer it to another cryptocurrency wallet or exchange.

STEP 3: VERIFY YOUR IDENTITY

Before you can withdraw your funds from Coinbase, you will need to verify your identity. This is to comply with KYC (know your customer) regulations and prevent fraud. To verify your identity, you will need to provide a government-issued ID and a selfie.

STEP 4: WITHDRAW YOUR FUNDS

Once your identity is verified, you can withdraw your funds from Coinbase. You will need to select your payout method and enter the amount you want to withdraw. If you are withdrawing to a bank account, you will need to provide your bank account information.

STEP 5: WAIT FOR YOUR FUNDS TO ARRIVE

After you have initiated your withdrawal, you will need to wait for your funds to arrive. The amount of time it takes for your funds to arrive depends on the payout method you have chosen. Bank transfers can take up to 5 business days, while PayPal transfers are usually instant.

Tips for Cashing Out from Coinbase

- Consider the fees: Coinbase charges fees for buying and selling cryptocurrency, as well as for withdrawing funds. Be sure to factor in these fees when calculating your profits.
- Choose the right payout method: Consider the fees and processing times when choosing your payout method. Bank transfers are usually the cheapest option, but they can take longer to process than other methods.
- Verify your identity in advance: If you're planning to cash out a large amount of cryptocurrency, it's a good idea to verify your identity in advance. This can save you time and prevent delays in the withdrawal process.
- Keep track of your transactions: It's important to keep a record of all your cryptocurrency transactions and withdrawals for tax purposes.

By following these steps and tips, you can successfully cash out your cryptocurrency on Coinbase and convert it to cash.

CHAPTER 2

How to Use LocalBitcoins to Find Buyers and Sell Your Crypto for Cash

LocalBitcoins is a peer-to-peer marketplace that allows you to buy and sell cryptocurrencies directly with other users in your area. It is a popular platform for those who want to sell their cryptocurrency for cash or other payment methods. Here's how you can use LocalBitcoins to find buyers and sell your crypto for cash:

STEP 1: CREATE AN ACCOUNT

The first step in using LocalBitcoins is to create an account. To do this, go to the LocalBitcoins website and click on the "Sign Up" button. You will need to provide your email address and create a password. Once you've done that, you will be sent a verification email to confirm your account.

STEP 2: SET UP YOUR PROFILE

After you have verified your account, you will need to set up your profile. This includes providing information about yourself, such as your name, location, and payment preferences. It's important to be honest and accurate when setting up your profile, as this will help you find potential buyers who match your criteria.

STEP 3: POST AN AD

The next step is to post an ad for the cryptocurrency you want to sell. To do this, go to the "Sell Bitcoins" page on LocalBitcoins and enter the amount you want to sell, the payment methods you accept, and the location where you want to meet your buyer. You can also set your own price or choose to sell at the current market rate.

STEP 4: FIND A BUYER

Once you've posted your ad, you will need to wait for a potential buyer to contact you. LocalBitcoins has a messaging system that allows you to communicate with buyers and negotiate the terms of the sale. It's important to be clear about your payment preferences and to verify the identity of your buyer before meeting in person.

STEP 5: MEET YOUR BUYER AND COMPLETE THE SALE

When you have found a buyer, it's time to meet in person and complete the sale. LocalBitcoins recommends meeting in a public place, such as a coffee shop or bank, and bringing a friend or family member with you for added security. Once you've received payment, you can transfer your cryptocurrency to the buyer's wallet.

Tips for Using LocalBitcoins

- Be cautious of scams: LocalBitcoins is a popular platform for scammers, so it's important to be cautious when dealing with potential buyers. Always verify the identity of your buyer and never release your cryptocurrency until you have received payment.
- Choose your payment methods wisely: LocalBitcoins allows you to choose from a variety of payment methods, including cash, bank transfer, and online payment systems. Be sure to choose a payment method that is secure and reliable.
- Check the market rate: When setting your price on LocalBitcoins, it's important to check the current market rate for your cryptocurrency. Setting a price that is too high or too low can deter potential buyers.
- Be patient: Selling your cryptocurrency on LocalBitcoins can take time, so be patient and persistent in your efforts.

By following these steps and tips, you can successfully use LocalBitcoins to find buyers and sell your crypto for cash. Remember to be cautious and verify the identity of your buyer before completing any transactions.

CHAPTER 3

Cashing Out from Binance: Tips and Tricks for Withdrawing Your Profits

Cashing out from Binance can be a straightforward process, but there are some tips and tricks to keep in mind to make sure you withdraw your profits safely and efficiently. Here are some key steps to consider:

1. Verify your identity: Binance requires users to complete a Know Your Customer (KYC) process before withdrawing funds. This involves providing a government-issued ID, such as a passport or driver's license, and proof of address. Make sure to complete this step before you plan to withdraw your profits to avoid any delays.
2. Choose the right withdrawal method: Binance offers several withdrawal methods, including bank transfer, credit/debit card, and third-party payment processors like PayPal. Each method has its own fees and processing times, so make sure to choose the one that's most convenient and cost-effective for you.
3. Check withdrawal limits: Binance has different withdrawal limits depending on your account level and the type of cryptocurrency you're withdrawing. Make sure to check these limits before making a withdrawal to avoid any issues.
4. Be aware of fees: Binance charges withdrawal fees for each transaction, and these fees can vary depending on the cryptocurrency and withdrawal method you choose. Make sure to check the fees before making a withdrawal and factor them into your profit calculations.
5. Consider using a stablecoin: If you're looking to cash out

your profits but don't want to convert them to fiat currency, consider using a stablecoin like USDT or USDC. These cryptocurrencies are pegged to the value of the US dollar and can be easily traded on other exchanges or used for online purchases.

6. Stay up-to-date on regulations: Cryptocurrency regulations can change quickly, so it's important to stay informed of any updates that could affect your ability to withdraw your profits. Keep an eye on news and updates from regulatory bodies in your country to avoid any surprises.

Overall, withdrawing your profits from Binance can be a simple process if you follow these tips and tricks. Make sure to choose the right withdrawal method, check fees and limits, and stay informed of any changes to regulations to ensure a smooth and hassle-free withdrawal process.

More Tips and Tricks for Using Binance

1. Use stop-limit orders: Binance offers stop-limit orders, which can be a helpful tool for minimizing losses or locking in profits. With a stop-limit order, you set a stop price and a limit price, and the order is triggered when the stop price is reached. This can be useful for automatically selling your cryptocurrency if the price drops below a certain level, or for taking profits if the price rises to a certain level.

2. Take advantage of margin trading: Binance also offers margin trading, which allows you to borrow funds to trade with more buying power. This can be a useful way to increase your profits, but it also comes with higher risks. Make sure to fully understand the risks and benefits of margin trading before using it.

3. Consider using Binance's native token, BNB: Binance's native token, BNB, can be used to pay for trading fees on the platform, and it also has several other use cases. Holding BNB can give you a discount on trading fees, and it's also used for token sales on the Binance Launchpad. If you plan to use Binance frequently, it may be worth considering holding some BNB to take advantage of these benefits.

4.   Be aware of security risks: Like any cryptocurrency exchange, Binance can be a target for hackers and other security threats. Make sure to enable two-factor authentication (2FA) on your account, use a strong and unique password, and never share your login details with anyone. It's also a good idea to withdraw your funds from the exchange and store them in a secure wallet when you're not actively trading.

By following these tips and tricks, you can make the most of your experience on Binance and avoid common pitfalls. Remember to always do your own research and stay informed of any changes to the platform or the broader cryptocurrency market to maximize your profits and minimize your risks.

Exchange Withdrawals

The time it takes to withdraw Bitcoin and other Cryptocurrencies from an exchange to your bank account can vary depending on a few factors, including the exchange's processing times, network congestion, and the specific bank you're using. Generally, it can take anywhere from a few hours to several days for the funds to appear in your bank account.

The process of withdrawing cryptocurrency from an exchange to your bank account typically involves several steps. First, you'll need to sell your Cryptocurrency on the exchange and convert it to your local currency. Then, you'll need to initiate a withdrawal request and provide your bank account information. The exchange will then process the request, which may involve some verification steps to ensure the withdrawal is legitimate. Once the withdrawal is processed by the exchange, the funds will be transferred to your bank account.

The time it takes for the exchange to process the withdrawal request can vary depending on the specific exchange you're using, as well as their processing times and any verification steps they may require. Some exchanges may process withdrawals in a matter of hours, while others may take several business days.

After the withdrawal is processed by the exchange, the time it takes for the funds to appear in your bank account can also vary depending on the specific bank you're using. In general, bank transfers can take several business days to complete, although some banks may offer faster transfer options for an additional fee.

Overall, the time it takes to withdraw Cryptocurrencies from an exchange to your bank account can vary depending on a range of factors. It's important to check the specific withdrawal policies and processing times of the exchange you're using, as well as the processing times and policies of your bank, to get a better idea of how long the transfer may take.

Banking Information

To withdraw Bitcoin from an exchange to your bank account, you typically need a standard checking account. You will need to provide the exchange with your bank account information, including the routing number and account number, so they can process the withdrawal and transfer the funds to your account.

It's important to note that some banks may have restrictions or fees associated with receiving transfers from cryptocurrency exchanges. It's a good idea to check with your bank to make sure they allow these types of transfers and to inquire about any potential fees before initiating a withdrawal.

Additionally, some exchanges may have specific requirements or restrictions on the types of bank accounts that can be used for withdrawals. For example, some exchanges may only allow withdrawals to bank accounts in certain countries or regions. It's important to review the exchange's withdrawal policies and requirements to ensure that you meet their criteria for withdrawals.

CHAPTER 4

Converting Crypto to Cash with PayPal: A Safe and Secure Option for Small

PayPal is a well-known and trusted payment platform that allows users to send and receive money online. In recent years, it has also become a popular option for converting cryptocurrency to cash, particularly for small transactions.

Here Are Some Steps to Follow When Converting Crypto to Cash With PayPal

1. Link your PayPal account to an exchange: To convert your cryptocurrency to cash using PayPal, you'll first need to link your PayPal account to a cryptocurrency exchange that supports PayPal withdrawals. Some popular options include Coinbase, BitPanda, and eToro.
2. Sell your cryptocurrency on the exchange: Once your account is linked, you can sell your cryptocurrency on the exchange and receive the funds in your exchange account. Be aware that there may be fees associated with selling and withdrawing cryptocurrency, as well as exchange rates to consider.
3. Withdraw your funds to PayPal: Once you've sold your cryptocurrency on the exchange, you can withdraw the funds to your linked PayPal account. Depending on the exchange, this process may take a few hours or a few days to complete.
4. Transfer the funds to your bank account: Once the funds are in your PayPal account, you can transfer them to your linked

bank account. This process typically takes a few business days, and there may be fees associated with transferring funds to your bank account.

One of the benefits of using PayPal to convert cryptocurrency to cash is the speed and convenience of the process. PayPal transactions are typically processed quickly, and you can access your funds almost immediately. Additionally, PayPal offers strong security measures to protect your account, such as two-factor authentication and fraud detection tools.

However, there are also some drawbacks to using PayPal for cryptocurrency transactions. PayPal fees can be relatively high, especially for international transactions or for transactions involving currency conversion. Additionally, PayPal has been known to freeze or limit accounts that are used for cryptocurrency transactions, so it's important to be aware of the risks and use caution when using this method.

Overall, PayPal can be a safe and secure option for converting cryptocurrency to cash for small transactions, but it's important to weigh the pros and cons and to consider alternative options for larger transactions or for those looking to minimize fees.

Here Are Some Additional Things to Consider When Using PayPal to Convert Cryptocurrency to Cash:

PayPal Policies and Restrictions

Before using PayPal to convert your cryptocurrency to cash, be sure to review the platform's policies and restrictions regarding cryptocurrency transactions. PayPal has been known to freeze or limit accounts that are used for cryptocurrency transactions, and some countries may have restrictions on using PayPal for this purpose.

1.   Fees: PayPal fees can be relatively high, especially

for international transactions or for transactions involving currency conversion. Be sure to factor in these fees when deciding whether to use PayPal to convert your cryptocurrency to cash.

2. Verification requirements: To use PayPal for cryptocurrency transactions, you may need to provide additional verification and documentation. This could include providing proof of identity, proof of address, and information about your cryptocurrency transactions.

3. Buyer and seller protections: PayPal offers strong buyer and seller protections for transactions processed through its platform, which can be helpful in mitigating the risk of fraud or disputes. However, be aware that these protections may not apply to all cryptocurrency transactions, and you may need to take additional precautions to protect yourself.

4. Alternatives: While PayPal can be a convenient option for converting small amounts of cryptocurrency to cash, there may be alternative options that offer lower fees or greater flexibility. For example, you may consider using a peer-to-peer marketplace like LocalBitcoins or a cryptocurrency debit card to withdraw cash directly from an ATM.

PayPal can be a safe and secure option for converting cryptocurrency to cash for small transactions, but it's important to be aware of the fees, policies, and restrictions involved. Consider weighing the pros and cons and exploring alternative options before deciding to use PayPal for your cryptocurrency transactions.

CHAPTER 5

How to Sell Your Crypto for Cash on P2P Marketplaces like Paxful and Bisq

Once you have decided to sell your crypto for cash on a P2P marketplace, there are a few steps you should follow to ensure a smooth and safe transaction. Here's what you need to know:

There are several P2P marketplaces available for buying and selling cryptocurrencies, and each platform has its own unique features and user base. Before choosing a platform, it's important to research and compare them based on factors like fees, security features, user reviews, and ease of use.

1. Set up an account: Once you have chosen a platform, create an account and verify your identity. This process typically involves providing personal information like your name, address, and email, as well as verifying your identity by uploading a government-issued ID or passport. The verification process may take some time, so be patient.
2. List your offer: After creating an account, list your offer to sell your crypto for cash. You'll need to specify the type of cryptocurrency you are selling, the amount, and the payment method you prefer. Some P2P marketplaces also allow you to set a minimum or maximum transaction amount, or choose whether to sell to buyers within your country or globally.
3. Wait for a buyer: Once your offer is listed, you'll need to wait for a buyer to accept it. This could take a few minutes or several hours, depending on the demand for your cryptocurrency and the competition from other sellers.

4. Communicate with the buyer: When a buyer accepts your offer, communicate with them to agree on the details of the transaction. This may involve verifying their identity by asking for their name, location, and a photo of themselves holding their ID or a sign with your username. You should also agree on the payment method, which could be cash deposit, bank transfer, or a digital payment app like PayPal or Venmo. Make sure you understand the risks and fees associated with each payment method, and be prepared to provide instructions on how to complete the payment.

5. Complete the transaction: Once you have agreed on the details, complete the transaction by sending the cryptocurrency to the buyer and receiving payment in cash or through the agreed payment method. It's important to follow the instructions carefully and double-check the transaction details to avoid mistakes. If you're meeting the buyer in person, make sure to choose a safe and public location, and bring a friend or family member with you if possible.

6. Leave feedback: After the transaction is complete, leave feedback for the buyer and the P2P marketplace. This helps build your reputation as a trustworthy seller and helps other users make informed decisions. Similarly, make sure to read the feedback left by other users before buying or selling on the platform, as this can give you valuable insights into their experience and reliability.

Overall, selling your crypto for cash on a P2P marketplace can be a profitable and convenient way to access your funds, but it's important to be cautious and informed about the risks involved. By following these tips and best practices, you can minimize the risks and ensure a successful transaction.

Pros and Cons of Cashing Out

When new traders are trying to cash out their cryptocurrency on P2P marketplaces, there are several things to be wary of. Here are some of the pros and cons of using P2P marketplaces for cashing out, as well as some potential risks to watch out for:

Pros:

- Quick and easy access to cash: P2P marketplaces offer a fast and convenient way to sell your cryptocurrency and receive cash, which can be useful if you need the money quickly.
- Competitive pricing: Because P2P marketplaces allow buyers and sellers to set their own prices, you may be able to sell your cryptocurrency for a higher price than on a traditional exchange.
- Decentralized and anonymous: P2P marketplaces are decentralized, which means that they are not owned or controlled by any central authority. This can provide a degree of anonymity and privacy, which may be desirable for some traders.

Cons:

- High fees: P2P marketplaces often charge higher fees than traditional exchanges, which can eat into your profits. Make sure to check the fee structure of the marketplace you're using and factor in the fees when setting your selling price.
- Scams and fraud: P2P marketplaces are vulnerable to scams and fraud, as it can be difficult to verify the identity and trustworthiness of other users. Be cautious of buyers who ask for unusual payment methods or seem too eager to complete the transaction.
- Market volatility: The price of cryptocurrency can be highly volatile, which means that the price you agree to sell at may change significantly before the transaction is completed. Make sure to factor in the potential price changes when setting your selling price and be prepared to adjust it if necessary.

Potential Risks:

- Payment fraud: Some buyers may use fraudulent payment methods, such as stolen credit cards or bank accounts, to buy cryptocurrency. Make sure to verify the legitimacy of the payment method before completing the transaction.
- Chargebacks: Some payment methods, such as PayPal, allow buyers to initiate chargebacks, which can reverse the payment even after the transaction is completed. Be cautious of using payment methods that are vulnerable to chargebacks.
- Money laundering: Some buyers may attempt to use P2P marketplaces to launder money or engage in other illegal activities. Be wary of buyers who are not transparent about their identity or payment methods.
- Hacking and security breaches: P2P marketplaces can be vulnerable to hacking and security breaches, which can result in the loss of your cryptocurrency or personal information. Make sure to use strong passwords and enable two-factor authentication to protect your account.

Overall, while P2P marketplaces can be a useful tool for cashing out cryptocurrency, they also carry a degree of risk. By being cautious, informed, and taking the necessary security measures, you can minimize the risks and maximize your profits.

CHAPTER 6

Cashing Out from Kraken: A Comprehensive Guide to Fiat Withdrawals

Kraken is one of the largest and most reputable cryptocurrency exchanges, and it offers a variety of options for cashing out your cryptocurrency holdings. Here is a comprehensive guide to fiat withdrawals from Kraken:

1. Verify your account: Before you can withdraw fiat currency from Kraken, you will need to verify your account. This involves providing Kraken with your personal information, such as your name, address, and government-issued ID.
2. Set up a fiat withdrawal method: Kraken offers several options for withdrawing fiat currency, including bank wire transfers, SEPA transfers, and SWIFT transfers. Choose the method that works best for you and follow the instructions to set it up.
3. Sell your cryptocurrency: Once your withdrawal method is set up, you can sell your cryptocurrency on Kraken and transfer the funds to your fiat account. Make sure to check the current market price of your cryptocurrency and set a selling price that will maximize your profits.
4. Initiate the withdrawal: Once you have sold your cryptocurrency, you can initiate the fiat withdrawal by going to the "Funding" section of your Kraken account and selecting your withdrawal method. Follow the instructions to enter the amount you wish to withdraw and any other required information.
5. Wait for the withdrawal to be processed: The processing time for fiat withdrawals from Kraken varies depending

on the withdrawal method you have chosen. Bank wire transfers typically take 1-5 business days, while SEPA transfers can take up to 2 business days. SWIFT transfers can take up to 10 business days.

6. Receive the funds in your fiat account: Once the withdrawal has been processed, the funds will be transferred to your fiat account. Make sure to check your account balance to confirm that the funds have been received.

When cashing out from Kraken, it's important to be aware of any fees that may be associated with your withdrawal method. Kraken charges a fee for most withdrawal methods, and the fees can vary depending on the specific method and currency you are withdrawing. Make sure to factor in the fees when setting your selling price and withdrawing your funds.

Overall, cashing out from Kraken can be a straightforward and secure process, as long as you take the necessary steps to verify your account and choose a reliable withdrawal method. By following the steps outlined above and keeping an eye on fees, you can convert your cryptocurrency holdings into fiat currency and access your funds in a timely and efficient manner.

Here are Some Additional Tips to Keep In Mind When Cashing Out From Kraken

Consider tax implications: Depending on where you live, cashing out your cryptocurrency holdings may have tax implications. Make sure to research the tax laws in your country and consult with a tax professional if necessary.

1. Check withdrawal limits: Kraken has withdrawal limits for fiat currency, which can vary depending on your account level and the currency you are withdrawing. Make sure to check the withdrawal limits for your specific account before initiating the withdrawal.
2. Verify your withdrawal address: Before initiating a

withdrawal, make sure to verify that the withdrawal address is correct. Kraken has a feature that allows you to verify withdrawal addresses, which can help prevent errors or fraudulent activity.

3.   Be patient: Fiat withdrawals from Kraken can take several days to process, so make sure to allow for enough time for the funds to be transferred to your account. Keep in mind that processing times can be longer during weekends and holidays.

4.   Monitor your account: After initiating a withdrawal, make sure to monitor your Kraken account and fiat account to ensure that the funds are transferred correctly. If you notice any issues or discrepancies, contact Kraken support as soon as possible.

Overall, cashing out from Kraken can be a convenient and secure way to access your cryptocurrency funds. By following the steps outlined in the previous answer, as well as the additional tips listed above, you can ensure a smooth and hassle-free withdrawal process.

CHAPTER 7

The Best Crypto Debit Cards for Instant Cash Withdrawals Anywhere in the World

Crypto debit cards have become increasingly popular in recent years as they offer a convenient way to spend your cryptocurrency holdings in the real world. Here are some of the best crypto debit cards available for instant cash withdrawals anywhere in the world:

1.   **Coinbase Card:** The Coinbase Card is a Visa debit card that allows you to spend your cryptocurrency holdings wherever Visa is accepted. You can use the card to withdraw cash from ATMs, as well as to make purchases online and in-store. The card supports several cryptocurrencies, including Bitcoin, Ethereum, and Litecoin.
2.   **Binance Card**: The Binance Card is a Visa debit card that allows you to spend your cryptocurrency holdings at over 60 million merchants worldwide. You can also use the card to withdraw cash from ATMs. The card supports several cryptocurrencies, including Bitcoin, Ethereum, and Binance Coin.
3.   **Wirex Card**: The Wirex Card is a Visa debit card that allows you to spend your cryptocurrency holdings at over 54 million merchants worldwide. You can also use the card to withdraw cash from ATMs. The card supports several cryptocurrencies, including Bitcoin, Ethereum, Litecoin, and XRP.
4.   **BlockFi Card:** The BlockFi Card is a Visa credit card that allows you to earn Bitcoin on every purchase you make. You can use the card to withdraw cash from ATMs, as well as

to make purchases online and in-store. The card supports several cryptocurrencies, including Bitcoin, Ethereum, and Litecoin.

5. **Crypto.com Card**: The Crypto.com Card is a Visa debit card that allows you to spend your cryptocurrency holdings at over 60 million merchants worldwide. You can also use the card to withdraw cash from ATMs. The card supports several cryptocurrencies, including Bitcoin, Ethereum, and Crypto.com Coin.

Here Are Some Additional Details About Each Of The Crypto Debit Cards

The Coinbase Card is a Visa debit card that is available in select countries. You can use the card to spend your cryptocurrency holdings wherever Visa is accepted, and the card automatically converts your cryptocurrency to the local currency at the time of purchase. The card has no annual fee, but there are transaction fees for using the card. The supported cryptocurrencies include Bitcoin, Ethereum, Litecoin, and others.

The Binance Card is available in select countries. You can use the card to spend your cryptocurrency holdings at over 60 million merchants worldwide, and the card automatically converts your cryptocurrency to the local currency at the time of purchase. The card has no annual fee, but there are transaction fees for using the card. The supported cryptocurrencies include Bitcoin, Ethereum, Binance Coin, and others.

The Wirex Card is available in select countries. You can use the card to spend your cryptocurrency holdings at over 54 million merchants worldwide, and the card automatically converts your cryptocurrency to the local currency at the time of purchase. The card has no annual fee, but there are transaction fees for using the card. The supported cryptocurrencies include Bitcoin, Ethereum, Litecoin, XRP, and others.

BlockFi Card: is available in the US. You can use the card to earn Bitcoin on every purchase you make, and the card offers rewards of up to 1.5% back in Bitcoin. The card has an annual fee, but there are no transaction fees for using the card. The supported cryptocurrencies include Bitcoin, Ethereum, and Litecoin.

Crypto.com Card: is available in select countries. You can use the card to spend your cryptocurrency holdings at over 60 million merchants worldwide, and the card automatically converts your cryptocurrency to the local currency at the time of purchase. The card has no annual fee, but there are transaction fees for using the card. The supported cryptocurrencies include Bitcoin, Ethereum, Crypto.com Coin, and others.

When choosing a crypto debit card, it's important to consider factors such as fees, supported cryptocurrencies, and availability in your country. Make sure to research the options available to you and compare the features and benefits of each card before making a decision.

Overall, crypto debit cards can be a convenient and secure way to access your cryptocurrency holdings and spend them in the real world. By choosing one of the best crypto debit cards available, you can enjoy instant cash withdrawals anywhere in the world and take advantage of the many benefits of using cryptocurrency as a payment method.

CHAPTER 8

Using Over-the-Counter (OTC) Trading Desks to Cash Out Large Amounts of Crypto

Over-the-counter (OTC) trading desks are platforms that allow large volume traders to buy or sell cryptocurrency without going through a traditional exchange. OTC trading is particularly useful for individuals or institutions looking to cash out large amounts of crypto, as it offers higher liquidity, faster execution times, and greater privacy than traditional exchanges. In this chapter, we'll discuss how to use OTC trading desks to cash out large amounts of crypto and the advantages and disadvantages of this approach.

What is OTC Trading?

Over-the-counter (OTC) trading is the process of buying or selling assets directly with another party, rather than through an exchange. OTC trading desks provide a platform for buyers and sellers to connect and execute trades at negotiated prices. OTC trading is often used by large volume traders who require faster execution times, higher liquidity, and greater privacy than traditional exchanges can offer.

OTC trading desks typically require minimum trade sizes in order to participate, which can range from tens of thousands to millions of dollars. This means that OTC trading is generally only accessible to high net worth individuals and institutions, and not suitable for smaller trades.

Using an OTC trading desk to cash out large amounts of crypto has several advantages

1. High liquidity: OTC trading desks offer high liquidity, which means that large trades can be executed quickly and efficiently. This is particularly useful for individuals or institutions looking to cash out large amounts of crypto quickly.
2. Faster execution times: OTC trades can be executed much faster than trades on traditional exchanges. This is because OTC trades are typically conducted directly between the buyer and seller, rather than being routed through an exchange.
3. Greater privacy: OTC trading offers greater privacy than trading on traditional exchanges. This is because OTC trades are conducted directly between the buyer and seller, without the need for the trade to be publicly listed on an exchange.
4. Negotiable prices: OTC trades are conducted at negotiated prices, rather than at the current market price. This means that buyers and sellers can agree on a price that is more favorable to them than the current market price.
5. Reduced price slippage: OTC trading can help to reduce price slippage, which is the difference between the expected price of a trade and the actual price at which the trade is executed. This is because OTC trades are typically executed with a single counterparty, rather than being routed through multiple exchanges, which can lead to price slippage.

Disadvantages of OTC Trading for Cashing Out Crypto

While there are several advantages to using an OTC trading desk to cash out large amounts of crypto, there are also some disadvantages to consider, including:

1. High fees: OTC trading desks typically charge higher fees than traditional exchanges. This is because OTC trades require a higher level of service and support, and are typically executed with a single counterparty, rather than being routed through multiple exchanges.
2. Counterparty risk: OTC trading involves counterparty risk, which is the risk that the other party will default on the trade. This risk can be mitigated by using reputable and well-established OTC trading desks with a proven track record.
3. Limited access: OTC trading is generally only accessible to high net worth individuals and institutions, as it requires minimum trade sizes that can range from tens of thousands to millions of dollars.
4. Lack of transparency: OTC trades are conducted directly between the buyer and seller, without the need for the trade to be publicly listed on an exchange. This lack of transparency can make it difficult to determine the true market value of the asset being traded.

How to Use an OTC Trading Desk to Cash Out Crypto

If you've decided to use an OTC trading desk to cash out your crypto, here are the general steps you can follow:

1.   Find a reputable OTC trading desk: Look for an OTC trading desk that has a good reputation in the industry, is well-established, and has a track record of successfully executing large trades. You can do this by searching online or asking for recommendations from other traders in your network.
2.   Contact the OTC trading desk: Once you've found an OTC trading desk that you're interested in using, contact them to discuss your requirements. You'll likely need to provide details about the amount of crypto you want to sell, the currency you want to receive, and the timeline for the trade.
3.   Negotiate the price: OTC trades are conducted at negotiated prices, rather than at the current market price. This means that you'll need to negotiate the price with the OTC trading desk. Be prepared to provide evidence to support your valuation of the crypto you want to sell.
4.   Agree on the trade terms: Once you've negotiated the price, you'll need to agree on the trade terms with the OTC trading desk. This will include details such as the currency you'll receive in exchange for your crypto, the payment method, and the timeline for the trade.
5.   Execute the trade: Once you've agreed on the trade terms, you can execute the trade. The OTC trading desk will transfer the agreed-upon currency to your account in exchange for your crypto.
6.   Transfer the currency to your bank account: Once you've received the currency, you'll need to transfer it to your bank account. This can be done through a wire transfer or other payment method, depending on the terms of the trade.

Overall, OTC trading can be a useful tool for individuals or institutions looking to cash out large amounts of crypto quickly and efficiently. However, it's important to understand the risks and benefits of this approach before using an OTC trading desk. It's also essential to do your due diligence and research different OTC trading desks before selecting one to use.

CHAPTER 9

How to Avoid Common Scams and Frauds When Cashing Out Your Crypto

Cashing out your crypto can be an exciting and profitable experience, but it's important to be aware of the potential risks involved. Here are some common scams and frauds to watch out for when cashing out your crypto:

1.   Phishing scams: These scams involve criminals posing as legitimate companies or websites in order to steal your personal information, such as login credentials or credit card details. To avoid phishing scams, make sure you only use trusted websites and never click on links from unknown sources.
2.   Fake exchanges: Some scammers create fake exchanges that look like legitimate platforms in order to steal your funds. To avoid fake exchanges, always research any exchange before using it and make sure it has a good reputation in the crypto community.
3.   Ponzi schemes: These scams involve a fraudulent investment scheme that promises high returns in exchange for investing in a particular crypto project. To avoid Ponzi schemes, be wary of any investment opportunity that promises unrealistic returns and do your own research to assess the legitimacy of the project.
4.   Fake wallets: Some scammers create fake wallets that look like legitimate wallets in order to steal your funds. To avoid fake wallets, always download wallets from official sources and make sure to only use wallets that have a good reputation in the crypto community.

5.   Malware attacks: Some scammers use malware attacks to steal your crypto or personal information. To avoid malware attacks, always use strong antivirus software and make sure to only download software from trusted sources.

6.   Social engineering: Some scammers use social engineering tactics to trick you into giving them your personal information or access to your crypto. To avoid social engineering, always be skeptical of unsolicited messages or requests and never give out your personal information or access to your crypto to anyone you don't trust.

In addition to being aware of these common scams and frauds, there are also some general best practices you can follow to help protect yourself when cashing out your crypto. These include:

1.   Only use trusted and reputable exchanges or marketplaces to cash out your crypto.

2.   Never give out your personal information or access to your crypto to anyone you don't trust.

3.   Use strong passwords and two-factor authentication to protect your accounts.

4.   Keep your private keys and seed phrases safe and secure.

5.   Be wary of any investment opportunity that promises unrealistic returns or seems too good to be true.

By following these best practices and being aware of the potential risks involved, you can help protect yourself from scams and frauds when cashing out your crypto.

Here Are Some Additional Details On How To Avoid Common Scams and Frauds When Cashing Out Your Crypto:

1.   Research the Exchange or Marketplace: Before using any exchange or marketplace to cash out your crypto, be sure to research the platform thoroughly. Check reviews and ratings from other users and look for any reports of fraud or scams associated with the platform. If possible, try to use

a platform that is regulated or has a good reputation in the crypto community.

2. Verify Email and Website Addresses: Be cautious of emails or messages that ask you to click on a link or provide personal information. Scammers often create fake websites and emails that look like legitimate ones to trick users into giving away their information. Check that the website address and email address are legitimate before entering any sensitive information.

3. Use Two-Factor Authentication: Two-factor authentication adds an extra layer of security to your accounts by requiring you to enter a code or use a biometric authentication method in addition to your password. Make sure to enable two-factor authentication on all of your accounts to help protect against unauthorized access.

4. Keep Your Private Keys Secure: Private keys are used to access your crypto assets and should never be shared with anyone. Keep your private keys secure by storing them offline in a hardware wallet or on a piece of paper in a safe place.

5. Avoid Suspicious Investment Opportunities: Scammers often use high-pressure tactics to lure victims into investing in fraudulent schemes. Be wary of any investment opportunities that promise high returns with little or no risk, as these are often too good to be true.

6. Use Reputable Wallets: Wallets are used to store your crypto assets and should be chosen carefully. Use reputable wallets that have a good reputation in the crypto community and make sure to keep your wallet software up to date with the latest security patches.

By following these tips and being aware of the potential risks involved, you can help protect yourself from scams and frauds when cashing out your crypto. Remember to always be cautious and never provide personal information or access to your crypto to anyone you don't trust.

Avoiding Scams and Frauds When Cashing Out Your Crypto:

1. Be Cautious of Unusual Requests: Be wary of any request

that seems unusual or suspicious. For example, if someone asks you to send them your crypto assets in exchange for a promised payment later, this is likely a scam. Similarly, be cautious of any request to send money to a third party or to use a specific payment method.

2. Use Common Sense: Use common sense when assessing investment opportunities or requests for your personal information. If something seems too good to be true, it likely is. Similarly, if someone is asking for information that seems unnecessary or overly invasive, it may be a red flag.

3. Educate Yourself: The more you know about the crypto industry and the risks associated with it, the better prepared you will be to avoid scams and frauds. Educate yourself on the latest scams and frauds in the industry and stay informed on best practices for keeping your crypto assets secure.

4. Use Regulated Platforms: Using regulated platforms can provide an extra layer of protection against scams and frauds. Regulated exchanges and marketplaces are required to follow certain guidelines and regulations to help protect users.

5. Keep Your Software Up to Date: Keeping your software up to date with the latest security patches can help protect against vulnerabilities that scammers may exploit.

6. Be Careful with Public Wi-Fi: When accessing your crypto accounts or making transactions, be cautious when using public Wi-Fi networks. Public Wi-Fi networks can be vulnerable to hacking and can be used by scammers to intercept your personal information.

7. Report Suspicious Activity: If you suspect that you have been the victim of a scam or fraud, report it to the appropriate authorities immediately. This can help prevent others from falling victim to the same scam.

By being vigilant and cautious, educating yourself on the risks associated with the crypto industry, and using trusted platforms and best practices, you can help protect yourself from scams and frauds when cashing out your crypto.

If you have been the victim of a scam or fraud when cashing out your crypto, it is important to take action as soon as possible to limit the damage and protect your assets.

Here Are The Steps You Should Take If You Get Scammed

Stop Any Further Transactions: If you suspect that you have been scammed, stop any further transactions immediately to prevent further losses.

1.   **Report the Scam**: Report the scam to the appropriate authorities, such as your local law enforcement agency or the Federal Trade Commission. Be sure to provide as much information as possible, including any messages or emails from the scammer and any transaction details.
2.   **Contact the Platform**: If the scam occurred on a crypto exchange or marketplace, contact the platform immediately to report the fraud and request assistance in recovering your assets.
3.   **Change Your Passwords**: Change your passwords for all of your accounts, including your email, crypto exchange accounts, and any other accounts that may be linked to your crypto assets.
4.   **Monitor Your Accounts**: Monitor your accounts closely for any unusual activity and report any suspicious transactions to the appropriate authorities.
5.   **Take Legal Action**: If the scammer is identified and can be located, you may consider taking legal action to recover your assets. Consult with a lawyer or other legal professional to explore your options.

Remember, the best way to protect yourself from scams and frauds is to be vigilant, educate yourself on the risks associated with the crypto industry, and use trusted platforms and best practices when cashing out your cryptocurrency

CHAPTER 10

Cashing Out Your Crypto At ATM's

Cryptocurrencies have gained widespread popularity over the years, with their values skyrocketing in some cases. Many people have invested in cryptocurrencies with the hope of making a significant profit. However, as with any investment, there comes a time when one needs to cash out. Cashing out cryptocurrency for cash can have its advantages and disadvantages. In this chapter, we will explore the pros and cons of cashing out crypto for cash.

Pros:

1. Liquidity: Cashing out crypto for cash provides you with instant liquidity. You can quickly convert your digital assets into cash, which is a widely accepted medium of exchange.
2. Convenience: Cryptocurrency exchanges have made it easier to cash out your digital assets. All you need is to link your exchange account with your bank account, and you can quickly transfer funds between them.
3. Stability: The value of cryptocurrencies can be highly volatile, and this volatility can cause significant fluctuations in your portfolio. Cashing out your crypto for cash can help to reduce this volatility and provide you with a stable store of value.
4. Taxation: Cashing out your cryptocurrency can help you manage your taxes. You will need to pay taxes on any

gains you make from the sale of your cryptocurrency, but cashing out can help you to calculate your tax obligations and reduce your tax liability.

Cons:

1. Potential Losses: Cashing out your cryptocurrency for cash means you are selling your digital assets at the current market value. If the value of your crypto rises after you have sold it, you will have missed out on potential gains.
2. Transaction Fees: Most cryptocurrency exchanges charge a transaction fee for cashing out your crypto. These fees can add up and reduce the overall amount of cash you receive.
3. Privacy: Cashing out your cryptocurrency for cash can compromise your privacy. You will need to link your exchange account with your bank account, which can expose your financial details to third parties.
4. Security: Cashing out your cryptocurrency for cash requires you to trust the exchange and the banking system. If either of these systems is compromised, you could lose your assets.

Conclusion:

Cashing out cryptocurrency for cash can be a useful strategy for managing your digital assets. It provides you with liquidity, stability, and convenience. However, it also has its disadvantages, such as potential losses, transaction fees, compromised privacy, and security risks. Before cashing out your crypto, you should weigh the pros and cons and consider your financial goals and risk tolerance. It's also essential to do your due diligence and research different cryptocurrency exchanges to find the most reputable and secure one.

Here Are 10 Cash Out Strategies You Can Use to Convert Your Cryptocurrency Into Cash

1. Direct bank transfer: You can transfer the funds from your cryptocurrency exchange account directly to your bank account. This is one of the most common ways to cash out.
2. PayPal transfer: Some exchanges allow you to transfer your funds to your PayPal account, which you can then withdraw to your bank account or use to make purchases.
3. Cryptocurrency ATM: You can use a cryptocurrency ATM to withdraw cash directly using your digital wallet.
4. P2P exchange: You can sell your cryptocurrency to other people directly using a P2P exchange platform like LocalBitcoins.
5. Cryptocurrency debit card: You can use a cryptocurrency debit card to make purchases or withdraw cash from an ATM.
6. Gift cards: You can sell your cryptocurrency for gift cards that you can use to make purchases at various retailers.
7. Over-the-counter (OTC) trading: You can sell your cryptocurrency to a buyer directly using an OTC trading platform like Coinbase OTC.
8. Online payment platforms: You can use online payment platforms like Skrill, Neteller, or Payeer to withdraw your funds to your bank account.
9. Trading for other cryptocurrencies: You can trade your cryptocurrency for other cryptocurrencies that are more stable or have a higher value, which you can then sell for cash.
10. Peer-to-peer lending: You can use a peer-to-peer lending platform to lend your cryptocurrency to others and earn interest, which you can then withdraw as cash.

Legal Age Requirements

The age requirements for transferring funds or conducting transactions can vary depending on the laws and regulations of the country or region where you are located, as well as the policies of the specific financial institution or service you are using.

In many countries, there are legal age requirements for financial transactions. For example, in the United States, the legal age for entering into contracts is 18 years old. This means that minors under the age of 18 cannot legally sign contracts, including those related to financial transactions, without the consent of a parent or legal guardian.

Furthermore, some financial institutions or payment processors may have their own age policies in place. For example, PayPal's User Agreement states that users must be at least 18 years old to use their services. Similarly, some cryptocurrency exchanges may have age restrictions in place to comply with local laws and regulations.

It's important to check the policies and regulations in your country or region, as well as the terms and conditions of the financial institution or service you are using, to ensure that you are eligible to conduct financial transactions. If you are under the legal age limit, you may need to have the consent of a parent or legal guardian to open an account or conduct financial transactions.

CHAPTER 11

The Pros and Cons of Cashing Out Crypto for Cash

When it comes to cashing out your cryptocurrency for fiat currency, there are both advantages and disadvantages to consider. In this chapter, we'll explore the pros and cons of converting your digital assets to cash.

Pros:

1.   Liquidity: One of the biggest advantages of cashing out your crypto is the immediate access to cash. This can be especially useful in times of financial need or when you want to make a purchase that requires fiat currency.
2.   Reduced Volatility Risk: Cryptocurrencies are notoriously volatile and subject to sudden price swings. Converting your crypto to cash reduces your exposure to this risk, as you'll be holding a more stable asset.
3.   Diversification: By cashing out some of your crypto holdings, you can diversify your investment portfolio and reduce your overall risk. This can be a smart move for those who are heavily invested in cryptocurrency.
4.   Simplification: If you find managing your crypto assets to be complicated or time-consuming, cashing out can simplify things. With cash in hand, you won't need to worry about managing digital wallets or keeping up with market trends.

Cons:

1. Tax Implications: As discussed in Chapter 12, cashing out crypto can trigger tax obligations. Depending on your jurisdiction, you may need to pay capital gains tax on your profits, which can be a significant expense.
2. Exchange Fees: When you convert your crypto to cash, you'll likely need to pay fees to the exchange or service provider. These fees can vary widely and may eat into your profits.
3. Time and Hassle: Cashing out can be a time-consuming and potentially complicated process, especially if you're dealing with large amounts of cryptocurrency. It may require multiple steps and verifications, which can be a hassle.
4. Missed Opportunities: The value of cryptocurrencies can fluctuate rapidly, and by cashing out, you may miss out on potential gains if the market continues to rise.

Ultimately, whether or not to cash out your crypto for cash is a personal decision that depends on your individual circumstances and investment goals. By weighing the pros and cons, you can make an informed choice that aligns with your financial strategy.

Pros:

1. Liquidity: Cryptocurrencies are often considered liquid assets because they can be difficult to convert to cash. By cashing out your crypto, you can access the liquidity of fiat currency, which can be useful for making purchases or covering unexpected expenses.
2. Reduced Volatility Risk: Cryptocurrencies are highly volatile, and their value can fluctuate dramatically in short periods of time. This can be both a blessing and a curse for investors, as it can lead to quick profits or large losses. By cashing out some of your crypto, it allows you to cash in some of the gains that you have made from your investments. This can be especially important if you have achieved significant profits

and want to receive those gains in a more tangible way.

3.   Diversification: By converting your crypto to cash, you can diversify your portfolio by investing in other assets such as stocks, bonds, or real estate. This can help to mitigate risk and create a more balanced investment portfolio.

4.   Tax Planning: Cashing out crypto can help you plan for tax purposes by allowing you to take advantage of losses and gains. If you have experienced a loss on your cryptocurrency investment, you can use that loss to offset gains in other areas of your portfolio. Conversely, if you have experienced a gain, you can cash out and pay taxes on your profits.

5.   Access to More Investment Opportunities: While cryptocurrencies have become more mainstream, many traditional investment opportunities are still only available in fiat currency. By cashing out your crypto, you can access a wider range of investment opportunities.

Cons:

1.   Fees: When you cash out your crypto, you will often have to pay fees to exchange the cryptocurrency for cash. These fees can add up quickly and eat into your profits.
2.   Tax Implications: Cashing out crypto can trigger tax implications, and it is important to understand the tax laws in your country or region. Depending on where you live, you may be required to pay capital gains tax on the profits from your investment.
3.   Security Risks: When you cash out your crypto, you may be putting yourself at risk of theft or fraud. This is especially true if you are using a third-party exchange or platform to sell your cryptocurrency. It is important to take precautions to protect your identity and your funds.
4.   Missed Opportunities: If you cash out your cryptocurrency too early, you may miss out on potential profits if the value of the cryptocurrency continues to rise. This is a common concern for many crypto investors, as the value of cryptocurrencies can be highly volatile and unpredictable.
5.   Lack of Privacy: If you are concerned about maintaining your privacy, cashing out crypto may not be the best option. When you exchange cryptocurrency for cash, you may be required to provide personal information to comply with anti-money laundering and know-your-customer regulations.

When Cashing Out Cryptocurrency, It Is Important To Be Cautious and Avoid Certain Actions That Can Put You At Risk. Here Are Some Things To Avoid When Cashing Out:

1.   Avoid using unsecured or unfamiliar platforms: Using unsecured or unfamiliar platforms to cash out your crypto

can put you at risk of fraud, identity theft, and loss of funds. Stick to well-established and reputable exchanges or platforms that have a proven track record of security and reliability.

2.   Don't rush the process: Cashing out can take time, and it is important to be patient and take the necessary steps to ensure the transaction is secure and completed correctly. Rushing the process can lead to mistakes or oversights that can result in loss of funds.

3.   Don't forget about taxes: Cashing out cryptocurrency can trigger tax implications, and it is important to understand the tax laws in your country or region. Failure to pay taxes on your cryptocurrency profits can result in penalties or legal action.

4.   Don't give out personal information: When cashing out your cryptocurrency, be wary of requests for personal information such as your social security number or driver's license. Providing this information can put you at risk of identity theft.

5.   Avoid making large transactions at once: Making large transactions at once can put you at risk of theft or fraud. It is important to take a cautious approach and make smaller transactions to reduce the risk of loss.

BLUEPRINT TO CASHING OUT CRYPTOCURRENCIES

6.   Don't forget to double-check your transaction details: Before completing a transaction, make sure to double-check all details to ensure accuracy. Mistakes can result in loss of funds, so it is important to take the time to review all transaction details before finalizing the transaction.

Here Is A Checklist Of Things To Do Correctly When Cashing Out Cryptocurrency:

1.   Choose a reputable platform: Select a reputable and secure platform to sell your cryptocurrency. Research the platform's history, user reviews, security features, and customer support before using it.
2.   Determine the best cash out option: Decide on the best cash out option for you, whether it's an exchange, peer-to-peer marketplace, ATM, or OTC trading desk. Consider the fees, transaction time, and security features of each option.
3.   Verify your identity: Most platforms require identity verification before allowing users to sell cryptocurrency. Prepare the necessary documents, such as your government-issued ID, proof of address, and proof of income, to avoid delays.
4.   Set up your payment method: Link your bank account, credit card, or PayPal account to the platform to receive your cash. Verify the payment method before initiating the transaction.
5.   Check the market price: Check the market price of your cryptocurrency before selling to ensure that you're getting a fair price. Monitor the price fluctuations and select the best time to sell.
6.   Calculate and prepare for taxes: Calculate the taxes you owe on your cryptocurrency gains and prepare to pay them. Consult a tax professional if you're unsure about the tax laws in your country or region.
7.   Start with small transactions: Start with small transactions

to test the platform's security and reliability before making larger transactions.

8. Review the transaction details: Double-check all transaction details, such as the amount, fees, and payment method, before finalizing the transaction.

9. Withdraw your cash: Withdraw your cash to your bank account or PayPal account and monitor the transaction until it's completed.

10. Secure your funds: Secure your funds by transferring them to a secure wallet or offline storage. Don't keep your cash in a platform's account for too long.

CHAPTER 12

Tax Implications of Cashing Out Crypto for Cash

Cashing out cryptocurrency for cash can have significant tax implications, and it's important to understand these implications before making any transactions. In this chapter, we will explore the tax considerations for cashing out cryptocurrency and provide some tips for minimizing your tax liability.

1. Cryptocurrency and Taxation

Cryptocurrency is considered a property by the Internal Revenue Service (IRS) in the United States, and any gains or losses from its sale or exchange are subject to capital gains tax. Capital gains tax is a tax on the profit made from the sale of an asset.

When you cash out your cryptocurrency for cash, you will need to calculate your capital gains or losses based on the fair market value of the cryptocurrency at the time of sale, less its cost basis (the original purchase price). If you have held the cryptocurrency for less than one year, the gains will be taxed at the short-term capital gains rate, which is the same as your ordinary income tax rate. If you have held the cryptocurrency for more than one year, the gains will be taxed at the long-term capital gains rate, which is typically lower than the short-term capital gains rate.

2. Tax Reporting

If you have sold or exchanged cryptocurrency during the year, you will need to report the transaction on your tax return. You will need to report the fair market value of the cryptocurrency at the time of sale or exchange, as well as its cost basis and the date of acquisition. The gains or losses from the transaction will be calculated based on this information.

The IRS requires that all taxpayers report any taxable cryptocurrency transactions on their tax returns, and failure to do so can result in penalties and interest charges.

3. Tax Planning

There Are Several Strategies You Can Use To Minimize Your Tax Liability When Cashing Out Cryptocurrency. Here Are A Few:

a. HODL: If you hold onto your cryptocurrency for more than one year before cashing out, you will be eligible for the long-term capital gains tax rate, which is typically lower than the short-term rate. This strategy is known as "HODLing," which stands for "hold on for dear life."

b. Tax-Loss Harvesting: If you have other cryptocurrency holdings that have lost value, you can sell those holdings to offset the gains from the sale of other cryptocurrency holdings. This strategy is known as tax-loss harvesting.

c. Gift or Donate: You can gift or donate your cryptocurrency holdings to a tax-exempt charity or non-profit organization to avoid paying capital gains tax on the transaction.

d. Consult a Tax Professional: If you have a significant amount of cryptocurrency to cash out, it may be worth consulting a tax professional to help you navigate the tax implications and find ways to minimize your tax liability.

4. Conclusion

Cashing out cryptocurrency for cash can have significant tax implications, and it's important to understand these implications before making any transactions. By knowing the tax rules and regulations, and planning ahead, you can minimize your tax liability and avoid any penalties or interest charges. Remember to report all taxable cryptocurrency transactions on your tax return and consult a tax professional if you have any questions or concerns.

When it comes to tax preparation for cryptocurrency transactions, it's important to work with a tax preparer who has experience and knowledge in this area. Not all tax preparers are familiar with cryptocurrency and the tax implications of buying, selling, and exchanging it.

Here Are Some Types Of Tax Preparers To Consider:

1. Certified Public Accountants (CPAs): CPAs are licensed professionals who have passed the Uniform CPA Exam and have met state licensing requirements. They can provide a range of tax services, including tax preparation, planning, and consulting. Many CPAs have experience in cryptocurrency taxation.
2. Enrolled Agents (EAs): EAs are tax professionals who have passed a rigorous exam and are authorized by the IRS to represent taxpayers in tax matters. They can provide tax preparation, planning, and representation services.
3. Tax Attorneys: Tax attorneys are lawyers who specialize in tax law and can provide tax planning, preparation, and representation services. They can be helpful in complex cases where legal advice is needed.

In terms of the amount of cryptocurrency that becomes taxable when you sell, any gains from the sale of cryptocurrency are subject to capital gains tax. This means that if you sell your cryptocurrency for more than you purchased it for, the difference is considered a capital gain and is taxable. The amount that becomes taxable is the difference between the sale price and the cost basis, which is the original purchase price.

For example, if you purchased 1 Bitcoin for $10,000 and then sold it for $50,000, you would have a capital gain of $40,000, which is the difference between the sale price and the cost basis. This $40,000 would be subject to capital gains tax.

It's important to keep accurate records of your cryptocurrency transactions, including the purchase price, date of purchase, sale price, and date of sale, to accurately calculate your capital gains or losses and minimize your tax liability.

As we conclude this book, we hope that you have gained a deeper understanding of the process of cashing out cryptocurrency for cash. We have covered the various methods of cashing out, the pros and cons of each, and the tax implications of cashing out cryptocurrency.

It's important to proceed with caution when cashing out cryptocurrency, especially when it comes to choosing a reputable exchange or cash-out method, as well as being mindful of potential tax implications. We recommend that you seek the advice of a tax professional before making any significant cash-out decisions.

Cryptocurrency is a dynamic and evolving space, and as such, we encourage you to continue your education and stay up-to-date with any changes in the industry. With a solid understanding of the various methods and considerations involved in cashing out cryptocurrency, you can make informed decisions that help you achieve your financial goals.

Thank you for reading this book, and we wish you success in your cryptocurrency endeavors.

Made in the USA
Las Vegas, NV
08 July 2023

74355410R00036